Fannie Lou Hamer

by Sandy Donovan

Raintree

Chicago, Illinois

For information, address the publisher:
Raintree, 100 N. LaSalle, Suite 1200, Chicago, IL 60602

Printed and bound in the United States at Lake Book Manufacturing, Inc.
07 06 05 04 03
10 9 8 7 6 5 4 3 2 1

Library of Congress Cataloging-in-Publication Data:

Donovan, Sandra, 1967-
  Fannie Lou Hamer / Sandra Donovan.
    v. cm. -- (African-American biographies)
Includes bibliographical references (p.) and index.
Contents: Introduction: a poor black woman -- Childhood in Mississippi -- Becoming an adult -- Married life -- Fighting for the right to vote -- More trouble -- Continuing the fight -- Fannie Lou Hamer's legacy -- Glossary -- Timeline.
  ISBN 0-7398-7030-0 -- ISBN 1-4109-0316-8 (pbk.)
  1. Hamer, Fannie Lou--Juvenile literature. 2. African American women civil rights workers--Biography--Juvenile literature. 3. African Americans--Biography--Juvenile literature. 4. Civil rights workers--United States--Biography--Juvenile literature. 5. Civil rights movements--United States--History--20th century--Juvenile literature. 6. Civil rights movements--Mississippi--History--20th century--Juvenile literature. 7. African Americans--Civil rights--History--20th century--Juvenile literature. 8. African Americans--Civil rights--Mississippi--History--20th century--Juvenile literature. 9. Mississippi--Race relations--Juvenile literature. [1. Hamer, Fannie Lou. 2. Civil rights workers. 3. African Americans--Biography. 4. Women--Biography.] I. Title. II. Series: African American biographies (Chicago, Ill.)
  E185.97.H35D66 2003
  973'.0496073'0092--dc21

                    2003001512

Acknowledgments
The publishers would like to thank the following for permission to reproduce photographs:
pp. 4, 6, 20, 42, 44, 47, 48, 50, 56 Bettmann/Corbis; pp. 8, 10, 14, 16, 24, 33, 36, 39, 49 Library of Congress; p. 22 Corbis; p. 26 George Ballis/Take Stock; pp. 28, 34 Flip Schulke/Corbis; pp. 40, 52 Associated Press, AP; p.55 Shelley Gazin/Corbis; p. 59 Townsend Davis.

Cover photograph: Bettmann/Corbis

Some words are shown in bold, **like this.** You can find out what they mean by looking in the glossary.

Contents

Civil rights leader Fannie Lou Hamer speaks out at a meeting for the rights of African Americans on August 22, 1964.

Introduction

Throughout most of the United States' history, African Americans were treated badly by white people. Until the 1960s, laws in most southern states kept black people **segregated,** or apart, from white people. African Americans were denied many rights and freedoms that are supposed to be enjoyed by all Americans. African Americans in the South were usually poor and did not have the opportunity to improve their lives.

In the 1950s and 1960s, that began to change. People across the country began working together to gain basic rights for African Americans. This work became known as the **Civil Rights Movement.** Most people have heard of civil rights leaders such as Dr. Martin Luther King Jr. Like many other leaders, King was African American, but he came from a **middle-class** family. He had had the opportunity to get an education. This gave him the knowledge and skills to fight for civil rights.

Fannie Lou Hamer enters the Democratic National Convention in Atlantic City, New Jersey, on August 25, 1964.

But other leaders of the **Civil Rights Movement** were poor women who had no education. Fannie Lou Townsend Hamer was one of them. She was born poor and only went to school for a few years. She often did not have enough to eat. She was treated badly and even beaten by white people many times in her life. She saw African Americans killed for no reason by white people.

Fannie Lou had every reason to be afraid of white people and do what they wanted. But she knew it was not fair that black people were treated badly. She refused to be afraid. When she learned that black people had the right to vote, she made up her mind to use that right. She fought the rest of her life to gain rights for African Americans.

In her own words

"I can say this: We need a change in Mississippi. I'm sick of being hungry, naked, and looking at my children and so many other children crying for bread."

"I believe that we have just got to keep some kind of faith that the people who want to make this country a good place to live can gain and influence politics in this country."

*A sharecropper stands in front of her family's home in Mississippi in 1937.
Sharecroppers farmed land for plantation owners for very little money.*

Chapter 1:
Childhood in Mississippi

Fannie Lou Townsend was the last of twenty children born to Jim and Lou Ella Townsend. She was born on October 6, 1917. Her family lived in a tiny shack in the country in Mississippi. She had fourteen older brothers and five older sisters.

Fannie Lou's grandparents had been slaves. By the time she was born, slavery had been outlawed in the United States for 50 years. But Fannie Lou's family did not live much better than slaves had lived. The Townsends were **sharecroppers.** This means they raised crops, but they had to share them with the landowner.

Sharecropping in Mississippi

Fannie Lou's family farmed a plot of land that was part of a large **plantation.** At one time, the plantation owner had owned many slaves to farm his land. When the slaves were freed after the Civil War (1861–1865), most of them had nowhere to go.

Fannie Lou grew up in a large sharecropper family much like this one. This sharecropper family worked on a plantation in Alabama in the 1930s.

The former slaves who stayed on the **plantation** became sharecroppers. They farmed land for the plantation owner. They were allowed to live on the plantation and grow crops, but they had to give some of their crops to the plantation owner. The rest they kept to feed their families. But the houses they lived in belonged to the plantation. They also had to buy all their supplies and the food they could not grow themselves from the plantation. It was too difficult for them to make a trip to another store to buy these things. They spent all of their time working in the fields.

By the time **sharecroppers** paid for items like sugar and flour, they had very little money left. They were never able to save enough money to buy their own land or build their own houses. They had to depend on the plantation owner for many things. In some ways it was like being a slave.

Difficult childhood

Fannie Lou's parents loved her and her brothers and sisters. They tried hard to make their children's lives happy. But Fannie Lou did not have an easy childhood. Her family's small wooden house had no electricity or running water. Some days they had only bread and onions for dinner. They hardly ever had enough to eat.

Fannie Lou's whole family worked all day. Fannie Lou started picking cotton when she was only six years old. Picking cotton was hard work. Cotton grows in hard little shells called bolls. Cotton pickers had to tear the cotton bolls from hundreds of plants a day. The bolls were sharp on the outside and often cut Fannie Lou's fingers.

Fannie Lou got a disease called polio when she was very young. Her family had no money for a doctor, and Fannie Lou was sick for many months. She recovered, but one of her legs did not grow properly. For the rest of her life, she walked with a limp.

Trying to make a better life

Fannie Lou's parents wanted to make their children's lives better. They wanted their children to go to school. But in those days not many Mississippi schools accepted black students. And the family needed everybody's help picking cotton.

In Montgomery County, where Fannie Lou lived, black children could only go to one school. This school was open only from December until March each year. These were the months when there were no crops to plant or pick. But they were also the coldest months. Even in the South, the temperature could get very cold in the winter.

Fannie Lou's family did not have enough clothes to keep them warm. Fannie Lou's mother tied rags around her children's feet in the winter. But they could not walk to school when it was too cold. They had to stay inside and try to keep warm in front of the fire.

Even though Fannie Lou only went to school for a few months a year, she learned to read and write. She won spelling bees. Most of all she loved to sing. At school she was one of the best singers. At home, she sang with her mother and listened to her mother sing to her. Her mother also sang to her as they worked in the cotton fields.

"This Little Light of Mine"

When Fannie Lou was a child, her mother often sang "This Little Light of Mine." It was an old African-American song that was often sung in church. The song became Fannie Lou's favorite. She often sang it when she found herself in trouble, and it became a favorite with many **civil rights** workers.

This little light of mine,
I'm gonna let it shine,
Oh, this little light of mine,
I'm gonna let it shine.
This little light of mine,
I'm gonna let it shine,
Let it shine, let it shine, let it shine.

All over Mississippi,
I'm gonna let it shine,
Oh, all over Mississippi,
I'm gonna let it shine.
All over Mississippi,
I'm gonna let it shine,
Let it shine, let it shine, let it shine.

Singers often add verses that they make up on the spot. A common verse during the **Civil Rights Movement** was "I've got the light of freedom, I'm gonna let it shine."

When Fannie Lou was young, not many Mississippi schools accepted black students. Here, a sharecropper woman teaches her children at home.

The family's own farm

When Fannie Lou was eleven, her parents finally had enough money to rent their own land. This meant they would not have to share their crops with the **plantation** owner. It meant they would have more money to buy food and clothes.

Fannie Lou's father bought three mules and two cows. He also bought some tools, including a plow. The mules could pull the plow through the fields to plant cotton. The family was very proud to own their own farm animals. These mules could plow the land so that crops could be planted and grown. They called the mules Ella, Bird, and Henry. Fannie Lou's father even saved enough money to buy a car. The family was happy. Finally, they were going to have enough to eat.

Then one day they woke up and found the mules lying on their sides. Someone had put poison in their food. All three of the mules had died. Without them, the family would not be able to grow their own crops. They had worked hard to get ahead, but it seemed like they never would.

During the Great Depression in the 1930s, millions of people lost their jobs and could not find work. These people line up in the hope of getting a five-cent meal.

Chapter 2:
Becoming an Adult

Fannie was thirteen when her family's mules were poisoned. They soon found out that a white neighbor had killed the animals. He was jealous that Fannie Lou's family was becoming successful. At that time, many white people did not want to see African Americans having any success.

Fannie Lou's family had to go back to **sharecropping.** Fannie Lou had to stop going to school. Her family needed her to work in the fields and help out at home. Fannie Lou was sad to leave school, but she knew she had to do what she could for her family.

More hard times

While Fannie Lou's family was going through hard times, people all around the country were also suffering. It was 1929, and the United States was entering the **Great Depression,** which lasted until 1939.

During the **Great Depression,** businesses across the country failed. Millions of people lost their life savings. There were no jobs and people could not find work. They lost their homes and could not feed their families.

The Great Depression made life hard for people of all races. But it made life particularly hard for black people in the South. White people had **discriminated** against them for a long time. **Discrimination** is treating people unfairly because they are different in some way. But during the Depression, some white men blamed African Americans when whites could not find jobs or afford to feed their families. This may have been why Fannie Lou's neighbor poisoned her family's mules.

Family life

Fannie Lou's family suffered during the Great Depression. After their mules were killed, they went back to **sharecropping.** But they could not pick enough cotton to feed the family. Fannie Lou and her brothers and sisters walked miles over frozen fields to gather scraps of cotton. They sold the scraps for a few cents.

Fannie Lou's mother often helped the neighbors kill their pigs. This was a job that most people did not want. But Fannie Lou's mother would take any job to help feed her family. To pay her, the

A six-year-old sharecropper

Sharecropping was common in the South after slavery ended. Under the sharecropping system, people who did not own land grew their crops on large **plantations.** They paid the plantation owner with a share of their crop. The plantation owners gained more from this system than the sharecroppers did. The sharecroppers barely had enough to eat. Because the landowners got part of the crop, they wanted the sharecroppers to grow as much as possible.

The owner of the plantation where Fannie Lou lived found her playing one day. She was six years old. He told her that if she picked 30 pounds of cotton, he would give her Cracker Jacks and canned fish from the store. To Fannie Lou, these were special treats that she could never afford.

So Fannie Lou went to the fields and picked 30 pounds of cotton. Then she went to the store and picked out her treat. But now the plantation owner knew she could pick cotton. He told her to go out every day and pick cotton with her family. He no longer bought her treats when she picked cotton. He expected her to work every day now. So Fannie Lou began working when she was six years old, and she worked hard for the rest of her life.

Larger cities in the North, such as Chicago, pictured here in 1940, often provided more job opportunities for African Americans than the South. Several of Fannie Lou's brothers and sisters moved to Chicago and other northern cities to find work.

neighbors gave her the pigs' heads and feet. She brought them home and made soup. This was often the only meat Fannie Lou ate all week.

Still, Fannie Lou's family tried to make the best of things. At night, they sometimes sat together and roasted peanuts for a special treat. They told jokes and sang. Then they went to sleep on cotton sacks stuffed with cornhusks.

Becoming an adult

Fannie Lou began to dream of doing something to help African Americans. She knew it was not fair that her family went hungry even though they worked all day. She was sad that her mother had to wear the same patched dress for years. She saw some white women wearing new clothes every day. She knew they did not work as hard as her mother.

Fannie Lou's father died in 1939, when Fannie Lou was 22. Her older brothers and sisters had begun getting married and moving away. Some of them moved to northern cities like Chicago, where they had a better chance of finding jobs. As the youngest child, Fannie Lou stayed home to be with her mother.

Soon after Fannie Lou's father died, her mother had an accident. She was chopping wood with an axe when a wood chip flew up and hit her in the eye. Her eye was swollen and bleeding, but she did not have the money to go to a doctor. Soon she lost her sight in that eye.

When Fannie Lou was 27, she married a man named Parry Hamer. Everyone called him Pap. He was 32. Fannie Lou's mother had recovered from her accident, and Fannie Lou was able to leave her and move to Pap's house after they were married. Now Fannie Lou Townsend became Fannie Lou Hamer.

Fannie Lou and her husband Perry worked on a plantation like this one shortly after they married. This was where the owner lived. The home Fannie Lou and Perry lived in was also on the property, but it was no where near as large or as nice.

Chapter 3: Married Life

Fannie Lou Hamer's new home was on a **plantation** in Sunflower County, Mississippi. It was about 4 miles (6.4 kilometers) from where she grew up. The nearest town was called Ruleville. Fannie Lou and her husband were also **sharecroppers.**

Fannie Lou liked her new home. The house had running water inside, and a bathtub. There was only cold water, but Fannie Lou heated water on the stove for baths.

Fannie Lou's new house also had a toilet inside, but it did not work. One day she asked the landowner to fix the toilet. He told her she did not need a toilet inside her house. Since Fannie Lou had never had an indoor toilet in her life, she did not argue.

But one day Fannie Lou went to clean the landowner's house. His house had two bathrooms, and Fannie Lou cleaned them both.

Workers pick cotton in a cotton field. Fannie Lou and her husband worked hard as sharecroppers in the cotton fields.

When she was cleaning the second one, the owner's daughter said not to worry about getting it too clean. She said it was the dog's bathroom. This man had a bathroom for his dog, Fannie Lou thought, but he did not think she should have a toilet. She was very angry about this.

Working three jobs

Fannie Lou knew it was not fair that her life was so difficult. But she could not see a way to change it. She continued to work hard. She always tried to make the best of her situation.

Now she had three jobs. She picked cotton in the fields and she was a timekeeper. This meant she kept track of how much cotton each worker picked. She also cleaned the boss's house.

Fannie Lou's husband worked hard, too. He picked cotton and drove a tractor at the farm.

A family of her own

Fannie Lou and her husband wanted to have a big family. They did not have much money, but they loved children. However, they were not able to have their own children.

The Hamers took care of any children who needed their help. They adopted one little girl who did not have a father and another little girl whose parents could not take care of her. This little girl had been badly burned when boiling water spilled from a tub.

Fannie Lou and her husband both worked from early in the morning until late at night. But they still found time to take care of their girls. They also helped other children. Fannie Lou's husband hunted rabbits and squirrels. He brought them home and Fannie Lou made stew. She made enough to feed anybody who came by.

In the evenings, Fannie Lou sang to her daughters. She sang the songs her mother had sung to her when she was young. She also sang songs she learned in church. All her life, Fannie Lou went to church and believed in God. She said this helped her get through her most difficult days.

Fannie Lou sings "This Little Light of Mine" at a civil rights meeting in 1964. She developed a love for singing songs she had learned in church as a young girl.

Learning her rights

Every Sunday, Fannie Lou went to church in Ruleville. She prayed that she would find a way to help her people. She had watched African Americans work hard and suffer her whole life. She wanted to find a way to make a difference.

One Sunday in 1962, when she was 44, she heard something in church that changed her life. **Civil rights** workers from the North were holding a big meeting the following night. Civil rights are the personal freedoms that are guaranteed to all U.S. citizens. These freedoms include the right to free speech, the right to choose a religion, and the right to vote.

Fannie Lou went to the meeting at church that night. She was amazed at what she heard. The civil rights workers said African Americans had the right to vote in elections. Fannie Lou had never voted. No black person she knew had ever voted.

The white people who ran Sunflower County did not want African Americans to vote. If African Americans voted, they might vote the whites out of office. For years, these whites had kept African Americans from voting by threatening them, sometimes even by killing them.

Everyone in the audience knew it was dangerous for a black person to try to vote. The civil rights workers asked if anyone was willing to try to **register** to vote. In the United States, citizens have to register, which means putting their names on a list, before they can vote. Most people were afraid. But Fannie Lou raised her hand.

An African-American woman raises her right hand swearing an oath during voter registration in 1966. Fannie Lou fought hard to gain the right for African-Americans to vote.

Chapter 4:
Fighting for the Right to Vote

Fannie Lou's life changed the day she raised her hand and said she would **register.** The law said that every U.S. citizen had the right to vote. But African Americans who tried to vote in Mississippi would face real danger. They might be beaten. They might lose their jobs. Their houses might be burned. They might be killed. They had many reasons to be afraid.

It was not easy for an African American to register, and Fannie Lou knew this. First, she would have to pass a reading test. White politicians used reading tests to keep African Americans from voting. They often used harder tests for black people than for whites. And in Mississippi, many African Americans had very little education. It was almost impossible for them to pass the reading test.

Even if a black person did pass the reading test, that was still not enough. They had to pay money to register. This was called a poll tax. If a 41-year-old black man wanted to register, he was often asked to pay twenty years of poll taxes. They charged him back taxes from when he was 21 years old. Most African Americans in Mississippi did not have enough money to pay this high tax.

Very few African Americans could pass the reading test and pay the high poll tax. Even when they did, though, it was still difficult to vote. Plenty of white people believed that black people were not as good as they were. Therefore, they believed that black people should not receive equal rights. They would do almost anything to keep African Americans from voting.

Some of these **racists** belonged to a group called the **Ku Klux Klan (KKK).** The Ku Klux Klan is an organization that believes white Christians are better than other people. Its members were known for wearing white robes and white hoods over their heads. They tried to keep black people from being treated as equals. At times they burned down their houses and churches. Sometimes they murdered African Americans.

Registering to vote

Fannie Lou knew that registering to vote would be difficult and dangerous. But she was determined to do it anyway. She wanted to help change the world around her. The **civil rights** workers asked people to come to the nearby city, Indianola, Mississippi. In

Rosa Parks

Like Fannie Lou, Rosa Parks was an ordinary African-American woman who stood up for her rights. Or, really, she sat down for her rights. In Montgomery, Alabama, in 1955, she was working as a department store clerk. Every day, she rode a bus to work in downtown Montgomery.

On Montgomery buses in the 1950s, black riders had to offer their seats to any white person who was standing. One day after work, Rosa was tired and her feet hurt. She was also tired of being treated badly by white people. So she kept sitting. The bus driver called the police, who came and took her to jail.

Leaders of the African-American community heard about her arrest. To protest the way Rosa Parks had been treated, they organized a bus **boycott**. A boycott is when a large group of people refuse to do something, such as ride the bus or shop at a store, in order to make a point. In 1955 in Montgomery, hundreds of African Americans refused to ride the buses. They said they would not ride until all paying bus riders were treated equally.

The bus boycott lasted for 382 days. The bus company lost a lot of money. Rosa Parks had to go to court for refusing to stand up on the bus. Almost one year later, the court agreed that the law was unfair. Bus drivers in Montgomery or anywhere else in the country could no longer make black riders stand. The boycott was called off and blacks began to ride the Montgomery buses again.

Rosa had achieved a lot by simply standing up for her rights. She became famous. She made friends with many civil rights leaders, including Dr. Martin Luther King Jr. She has given speeches and received many awards. One is the Presidential Medal of Freedom, given to her in 1996 by President Clinton. This is the highest honor given outside of the military in the United States.

Indianola, they would go to the courthouse to **register.** Fannie Lou told her husband about her decision. He knew he could not stop her, but he did not go with her.

On the morning of August 31, 1962, Fannie Lou met the **civil rights** workers in Ruleville. Seventeen other African Americans also showed up. That was more people than the civil rights workers had expected.

They rode on an old yellow bus to Indianola. When they arrived, many of the people were afraid of what might happen in the courthouse. They stood around outside, near the bus. But Fannie Lou walked proudly, with her head high and her shoulders back. She walked up the steps and into the courthouse. The others followed her.

Inside, Fannie Lou told the clerk that they had come to register. He spoke to her rudely. He told her that only two people could register at a time. So Fannie Lou and one man stayed inside while the others waited on the bus.

First they had to fill out a long form. They had to answer many questions, including who they worked for. Fannie Lou knew that if she answered this, her boss would find out she was trying to vote. She could lose her job. Her whole family would be in trouble. The **plantation** owner would be very angry and

In August 1962, Fannie Lou and seventeen other African Americans rode a bus like this one to the Indianola, Mississippi, courthouse to register to vote.

could throw them out of their home. But if she did not answer, she would not be able to register. So Fannie Lou answered all of the questions.

Then the clerk brought out a big black book. It was the Mississippi Constitution. Fannie Lou did not even know that Mississippi had a constitution. The clerk asked her to copy a long section from the book. Fannie Lou took her time and wrote carefully. She did not want to make any mistakes.

An African American woman reads a sample voting ballot in 1966. Civil rights leaders held classes to help new voters learn about the voting process.

Next the clerk asked her what the section she had copied meant. Fannie Lou did not know what it meant. It was written in "fancy" language that most people would not understand. And she had never seen it before. She failed the test, and so did the man with her.

Home to Ruleville

Fannie Lou was disappointed to fail the test, but she was proud that she had tried. She boarded the bus with the others for the drive back to Ruleville. It had already been a long day.

On the drive home, a police car pulled the bus over. The police said the bus was too yellow and arrested the driver. They took him back to Indianola.

With the driver gone, the people on the bus became afraid. They knew the bus had been pulled over only because they had tried to **register.** They began to worry about what would happen to them and their families. But Fannie Lou began to sing. She sang "This Little Light of Mine" in a clear, strong voice. Her singing made the people on the bus feel stronger and less afraid.

Soon the police brought the driver back to the bus. They fined him $30, but he did not have that much money. Everyone on the bus gave what money they had, and they came up with the $30. Finally they were free to drive back to Ruleville.

Fannie Lou was determined to fight for civil rights for African Americans. Here, she takes part in a civil rights march in Hattiesburg, Mississippi, in the early 1960s.

Chapter 5: More Trouble

Fannie Lou's troubles did not end when she returned home from Indianola. In fact, her life would never be the same again.

While Fannie Lou was stuck on the bus, her boss, the landowner, visited her husband. The boss said that he had heard Pap Hamer's wife was trying to **register** to vote. He told Pap to tell his wife to go back to Indianola and take her name off the list. If she did not, he said, she could not stay on his land anymore. The Hamers had lived there for 18 years.

When Fannie Lou got off the yellow bus in Ruleville, she walked home. When she heard what the boss wanted her to do, she said she did not care if he threw her off the **plantation.** She said she was going to stand up for her rights.

Fannie Lou packed a small bag. Her husband took her and their two daughters back to Ruleville. There they stayed at a friend's house in town.

Fannie Lou stayed at her friend's house for several days. The friend was brave to invite her. By now everyone in Ruleville had heard that Fannie Lou had tried to vote. Gunshots were fired at the house. White **racists** wanted to scare Fannie Lou into changing her mind about voting.

Pap was worried about his wife. He was proud of her, but he was afraid someone would kill her. He took her to live with relatives in another county. While Fannie Lou was there, some **civil rights** workers heard her story. They asked her if she would speak about her experiences to an audience.

Going public

Fannie Lou had never spoken before a large group of people. But she believed in the rights of all African Americans. When the civil rights workers invited her to come to a big meeting in Nashville, Tennessee, she agreed. The workers belonged to a group called the **Student Nonviolent Coordinating Committee (SNCC)**. This was a group of young black and white people who traveled around the South working for equal rights.

Members of the Student Nonviolent Coordinating Committee (SNCC) gather in Washington, D.C., in 1967 to speak out for equal rights. SNCC invited Fannie Lou to speak at a big meeting in Nashville, Tennessee.

Throughout her life, Fannie Lou spoke on behalf of African Americans in order to gain the rights they deserved.

Fannie Lou was 45 and she had never been outside of Mississippi. In Nashville she spoke to large crowds. She spoke to newspaper reporters. She talked about trying to **register** and being kicked out of her home by her boss. People thought Fannie Lou was very brave.

Soon Fannie Lou returned to Ruleville. Since she would not change her mind about voting, her husband was fired from his job. The family lost their home on the **plantation.** They soon rented a tiny house in Ruleville.

Fannie Lou went to work for **SNCC.** She traveled across Mississippi and Tennessee and helped people register to vote. She told her story to many groups of people. She worked as hard as she had worked in the cotton fields, but now she was working for freedom. And she still sang her favorite song, "This Little Light of Mine."

Meanwhile, Fannie Lou kept studying to pass the voting test. In January 1963, she finally passed. At age 45, she would finally be able to vote.

Arrested

On June 9, 1963, Fannie Lou was returning to Mississippi from a **civil rights** meeting in Tennessee. She was on a bus with other civil rights workers. They stopped at a bus station in Winona, Mississippi, wanting to use the rest room and buy food.

In August 1964, New Jersey police block Fannie Lou and members of the Mississippi Freedom Democratic Party from the Democratic National Convention. Fannie Lou and others wanted the country to know that African Americans were not allowed to vote in Mississippi.

But when some of them got off of the bus, the police would not let them go inside the station. They said it was for whites only. The police pushed and shouted at them. Soon the whole group was arrested.

At the jail, the police put Fannie Lou and the others in cells and beat them with long leather straps. They beat Fannie Lou so hard that her whole body was swollen and black and blue. She could not feel her arms.

Soon other **civil rights** workers heard about the arrest and came to the jail. The workers put up money, called bail, to free Fannie Lou and her friends. They had been beaten so badly that they all needed to go to a doctor.

Fannie Lou was angry, but she would not quit. She felt that she was doing the only thing she could to make her people's lives better. Fannie Lou and her friends decided to **sue** the police who beat them. This means they took them to court and accused them of breaking the law. In court, there was a **jury** trial, but the members of the jury were all white. They said that the police were not guilty of anything.

Fannie Lou, in the center of the photograph, consoles the parents of Michael Schwerner, one of three civil rights workers killed during the summer of 1964. They are protesting outside of the Convention Hall in Atlantic City, New Jersey, to demand members of the Freedom Party be allowed onto the convention floor. Michael is pictured on the sign. Mr. Schwerner is the man speaking.

Chapter 6:
Continuing the Fight

Soon, Fannie Lou was known all over the South. People heard about her arrest and beating. They knew she had lost her home and that she and her husband had lost their jobs. Many African Americans said she was an **inspiration** to them. This meant that she made them want to be as strong in their own lives as she was in hers.

Fannie Lou continued to work for SNCC, helping people register. She walked for miles across Mississippi, talking to sharecroppers and other poor African Americans. She was asked to speak at many meetings and **conventions.**

National work

In 1964, the United States was getting ready to elect a president. Fannie Lou and her fellow **civil rights** workers wanted as many African Americans as possible to register and vote. But they knew that it would not be possible to reach everyone. And they knew that most African Americans who tried to **register** to vote would not be allowed to.

Before presidential elections, each major **political party** holds a national **convention.** A political party is an organization that runs **candidates** in elections. The two major parties in the United States are the Democratic Party and the Republican Party.

Usually each state sends a **delegation,** or group of people, to each national convention. The delegations from Mississippi had always been completely white. They were supposed to represent the whole state of Mississippi, but they really only represented whites.

Civil rights workers wanted the whole country to understand that most African Americans were not allowed to vote in Mississippi. They wanted the country to know that most black people in Mississippi did not feel that the Mississippi Democratic Party spoke for them. So they formed a new political party, the Mississippi Freedom Democratic Party. This party had both white and black members.

New Jersey

In 1964 Fannie Lou went to the Democratic National Convention in Atlantic City, New Jersey. She was part of the Mississippi Freedom Democratic Party's delegation. They asked to represent

Fannie Lou speaks at the Democratic Convention in 1968 in Chicago, Illinois. This time, the convention let her party, the Mississippi Freedom Democratic Party, represent Mississippi.

Fannie Lou and other members of the Mississippi Freedom Democratic Party speak with delegates at the 1964 Democratic Convention.

the state of Mississippi. They wanted to replace the all-white Mississippi Democratic Party **delegation.**

The Democratic Party had to decide which delegation represented Mississippi. Many famous **civil rights** leaders, including Dr. Martin Luther King Jr., spoke to the Democratic Party. They argued that an all-white delegation could not represent the whole state. But the speaker everyone remembered later was Fannie Lou Hamer.

Andrew Young

Andrew Young was born in New Orleans, Louisiana in 1932. He was from a **middle-class** African-American family. He studied at all-black schools all the way through college.

In 1955 he became a minister. He began working for the right of blacks to vote in Mississippi. When Fannie Lou was arrested and beaten in Winona, Mississippi, in 1963, Andrew Young went to get her out of jail. Andrew and Fannie Lou stayed friends for the rest of Fannie Lou's life.

In 1972 Andrew was elected to the U.S. Congress from Georgia. He was reelected in 1974 and 1976. In 1976 President Jimmy Carter made Andrew the U.S. ambassador to the United Nations. As ambassador, he fought for human rights around the world. Many people did not agree with his ideas on human rights and he left his job as ambassador in 1979. In 1981 he was elected mayor of Atlanta. He was mayor until 1989. From 2000 until 2001, he was president of the National Council of Churches. Andrew Young continues to live in Atlanta.

In August 1965, Fannie Lou (left) and two other members of the Mississippi Freedom Democratic Party read a telegram from Congressional House Speaker John McCormick in front of the U.S. Capitol. The telegram gave Freedom Party members the permission to sit in on House debates about the legality of Mississippi's voting laws.

Fannie Lou talked about how African Americans across the South were kept from voting. She talked about being arrested and beaten by the police because she helped black people **register** to vote. Television and newspaper reporters recorded her words. People around the country were shocked to hear how badly she had been treated just for trying to vote. They were amazed at how brave she was. Thousands of people across the country wrote letters of support for Fannie Lou and her party.

But it was not enough. The Mississippi Freedom Democratic Party did not win its fight that year. The Democratic Party let the all-white **delegation** represent Mississippi. For two days, Fannie Lou tried to walk into the convention and take a seat. Each time, guards stopped her. But she made her point. When the guards stopped her from taking a seat, she began to sing. She sang "This Little Light of Mine" and "Go Tell It on the Mountain." People around the country saw her on the evening television news.

Continuing the fight

After the **convention,** Fannie Lou went home to Mississippi. She was sad and angry that her party had not been allowed to represent Mississippi. But she was still determined to gain voting rights for African Americans. She even ran for Congress that fall. She was the **candidate** of the Mississippi Freedom Democratic Party. She did not win, but more than 30,000 people voted for her.

Four years later, in 1968, another presidential election took place. Fannie Lou went to the Democratic Party convention in Chicago. But this time the convention allowed her party to represent Mississippi. They sent the all-white Mississippi delegation home. Everybody at the convention stood up and applauded when Fannie Lou took her seat. She had won a big battle for African Americans in Mississippi and around the country.

Fannie Lou speaks to a crowd of people at a civil rights rally in 1965.

Chapter 7:
Fannie Lou Hamer's Legacy

By the late 1960s, Fannie Lou was in poor health. She had never really recovered from her difficult childhood and from having polio. She also never fully recovered from being beaten by the police in 1963.

Fannie Lou was often tired and ill, but she continued to fight for rights for African Americans. She wanted younger African Americans to have an easier life than she had. She often said she was sick and tired of being sick and tired.

A sad year

Although Fannie Lou had won a big battle for African Americans, she knew that a lot more change was needed. In 1967 a sad event in her own life reminded her of this need.

In the spring of 1967, Fannie Lou's daughter Dorothy became sick. Fannie Lou took her to the local hospital, but they refused to treat her because she was black. Fannie Lou started to drive her to a hospital in Memphis, Tennessee, which was 127 miles (203 kilometers) away.

Dorothy died on the way to Memphis. She left two young daughters. Dorothy's husband had been wounded in the war in Vietnam and could not take care of the girls. So at the age of 50, Fannie Lou and her husband adopted their two grandchildren.

Helping the Poor

Fannie Lou's life had changed a great deal since she boarded that yellow bus in 1962. At the time, she had never been outside of Mississippi. Only a few years later, she was traveling around the country. People everywhere knew who Fannie Lou was. They wanted to hear her thoughts on the **civil rights** struggle. She even taught a class at Shaw University in Raleigh, North Carolina.

In 1969 Fannie Lou started a small business called the Freedom Farm Cooperative. She bought some farmland and helped poor people—both white and black—grow crops. She wanted to make sure that poor people would have enough to eat. She remembered too many times in her own life when she went hungry. The food grown on Freedom Farm helped feed 1,500 people.

Children participate in an activity with their teacher in a Head Start program. Fannie Lou helped bring the Head Start program to children in the Mississippi countryside.

Fannie Lou helped poor people in other ways, also. She helped bring the Head Start program to the Mississippi countryside. Under this program, children from poor families could begin school at age three. This helped them do well in school when they were older.

Fannie Lou worried about children from poor families who were left alone while their parents worked. In those days, most mothers did not hold jobs outside the home. They stayed home to take care of their children. But many poor mothers had to work

Fannie Lou was a respected civil rights leader who spoke in front of many audiences. Here, she is one of the speakers at the National Women's Political Caucus in July 1971.

long hours to buy food for their families. Fannie Lou helped start a child-care center so that their children would be taken care of while their mothers worked.

Housing for poor workers in Mississippi also worried Fannie Lou. She remembered what it was like to live in a house owned by someone else. At any time, the owner could throw the family out, as Fannie Lou's boss had done to her. So Fannie Lou joined a group called the Young World Developers. This group helped build houses for both African-American and white families in need.

Honors

During her lifetime, Fannie Lou received many honors. Many universities awarded her honorary degrees. An honorary degree is given to recognize important work a person has done, not because the person graduated from the university. Fannie Lou received honorary degrees from schools including Shaw University, Howard University, Morehouse College, and Columbia College in Chicago.

Fannie Lou received other honors from around the country. In 1969 she was invited to the White House for a conference on health and nutrition. In 1970 the high school in Ruleville, Mississippi, held Fannie Lou Hamer Day. Six years later, in 1976, the town of Ruleville celebrated Fannie Lou Hamer Day. Black and white people honored their famous resident together.

Fannie Lou Hamer was buried at this site in Ruleville, Mississippi, in March 1977.

By the 1970s, Fannie Lou had several illnesses. She often had to spend time in hospitals because she had a disease called diabetes, which made it hard for her body to fight infections. Her heart was also weak. Because of poverty she had had a poor diet and poor health care for most of her life. In 1976 she found she had breast cancer. She had an operation, but she did not fully recover. She died on March 14, 1977, in Mound Bayou, Mississippi. She was 59 years old.

People around the country mourned for Fannie Lou. They knew they had lost one of the nation's strongest **civil rights** fighters. Fannie Lou's actions had changed the lives of many African Americans. She had shown that all people are capable of using their lives for good. She had shown that being brave in the face of fear can bring about change.

At her funeral in Ruleville, many famous people from around the country spoke. The U.S. ambassador to the United Nations, Andrew Young, was one of the speakers. He told the crowded church, "None of us would have been where we are now had she not been there then." After he spoke, he led the church in singing "This Little Light of Mine."

Fannie Lou Hamer was buried near her daughter Dorothy in Ruleville. Her gravestone holds the words "I'm sick and tired of being sick and tired."

Glossary

candidates people who run for office in elections

civil rights personal freedoms that are guaranteed to all U.S. citizens

Civil Rights Movement organized struggle to gain full rights for African-Americans. It took place during the 1950s and 1960s.

conventions large, usually national or international meetings of people with similar interests. They can last several days.

delegation small group of people representing a larger group at a meeting. At national political conventions in the United States, each state sends a delegation.

discrimination treating a person unfairly because the person is different in some way

Great Depression period of time from 1929 to 1939 when millions of Americans lost their jobs and, because they had no money, their homes

inspiration person or event that makes other people want to do something equally good

jury group of men and women who decide whether a person on trial is innocent or guilty

Ku Klux Klan (KKK) organization that believes white Christians are better than other people. It sometimes burned African-American houses and churches and murdered African Americans.

middle class people who make an average amount of money. They are neither rich nor poor.

plantation very large farm that is worked by people who live on it but do not own it

political party group that runs candidates in elections, and helps run the government

racists people who dislike a whole group of people because of their race or color

register sign up for voting

segregate kept apart. A set of laws forced African Americans and whites in the South to live apart from each other.

sharecroppers people who farm land that someone else owns. The sharecropper has to give the landowner part of the crop and has a hard time earning a living.

Student Nonviolent Coordinating Committee (SNCC) group of young black and white people who worked for equal rights for African Americans in the 1960s

sue taking someone to court because he or she has acted in an illegal manner. If the person taken to court is found guilty, he or she will owe money.

Timeline

1917: Fannie Lou Townsend is born October 6 in Mississippi to a sharecropping family.

1928: Fannie Lou's parents rent their own land to farm.

1930: A neighbor poisons the family mules; Fannie Lou's family returns to **sharecropping.**

1939: Fannie Lou's father dies.

1944: Fannie Lou marries Pap Hamer; becomes Fannie Lou Hamer.

1962: Fannie Lou travels to Indianola, Mississippi, to register to vote; in response, the **plantation** owner makes her leave her home.

1963: Fannie Lou is arrested in Winona, Mississippi, and beaten by the police.

1964: Fannie Lou helps form the Mississippi Freedom Democratic Party; she travels to the Democratic National **Convention** in Atlantic City, New Jersey; she runs for Congress.

1967: Fannie Lou's daughter Dorothy dies.

1968: Fannie Lou wins a seat at the National Democratic Convention in Chicago.

1969: Fannie Lou starts the Freedom Farm Cooperative; she is invited to the White House for a conference on health and nutrition.

1970: Ruleville Central High School holds Fannie Lou Hamer Day.

1976: Town of Ruleville celebrates Fannie Lou Hamer Day.

1977: Fannie Lou dies in Mound Bayou, Mississippi, on March 14.

Further Information

Further reading

Altman, Susan. *Extraordinary African-Americans: From Colonial to Contemporary Times.* New York: Children's Press, 2001.

Meltzer, Milton. *There Comes a Time: The Struggle for Civil Rights.* New York: Random House, 2001.

Vernell, Marjorie. *Leaders of Black Civil Rights.* Farmington, Mich.: Gale Group, 2000.

Weber, Michael. *The African-American Civil Rights Movement.* Chicago: Raintree, 2001.

Addresses

To learn more about the history of Fannie Lou Hamer's voting and civil rights struggles:
The Fannie Lou Hamer Project
729 Academy Street
Kalamazoo, Michigan 49007

To find out more about Fannie Lou Hamer and other famous American women:
The National Women's Hall of Fame
76 Fall Street
Post Office Box 335
Seneca Falls, New York 13148

Index